Go Vegan!
It will be good for you,
good for the animals,
and good for the planet!

This book is dedicated to PETA

People for the

Ethical Treatment of Animals

www.peta.org

Strong Chord Progressions in Eagle 53

For Eagle 53 Tuned Musical Instruments

by
John O'Sullivan

Published by
Pan Music Publishing

ISBN 978-1-7394074-1-4

Contents

Introduction

This book describes a number of chord progressions that I deem to be strong when playing in the Eagle 53 Musical Tuning. I worked out Eagle 53 in 2016. I have since discovered that Eagle 53 is not new. It was proposed by the mathematician A.J Ellis (1814 - 1890). It has been called The Duodene in 53TET. What *is* new in this book (and my other music books) are my unique approaches to building strong chords, scales and chord progressions.

The chords and scales presented here should work on stringed instruments such as guitar, banjo, mandolin and piano. I'm not 100% sure but I think the chords and scales should work on wind instruments (e.g. pipe organs) as well. This has to do with different instruments having different timbres. I am not an expert on timbre but I suspect my chords and scales should be acceptable on *most* polyphonic instruments.

Here is an outline of the Eagle 53 tuning...
A standard semitone is 100 cents wide. A standard octave is 1200 cents wide. In the standard 12 Tone Equal Temperament the distance between any two notes is 100 cents. So if E is 0 cents then F is 100 cents, F# is 200 cents, G is 300 cents and so on.

Eagle 53 is tuned differently. I like to start on E. In Eagle 53 if E is 0 cents then F is 113.2 cents. Here are the cent values of each note in Eagle 53...

E	0	cents	1/1	
F	113.2	cents	16/15	approx
F#	203.8	cents	9/8	approx
G	317.0	cents	6/5	approx
G#	384.9	cents	5/4	approx
A	498.1	cents	4/3	approx
A#	588.7	cents	7/5	approx
B	701.9	cents	3/2	approx
C	815.1	cents	8/5	approx
C#	883.0	cents	5/3	approx
D	1018.9	cents	9/5	approx
D#	1086.8	cents	15/8	approx
E	1200	cents	2/1	

Check out my book: Eagle 53 My Ultimate Musical Tuning (3rd Edition) which describes how I worked out Eagle 53.

This book in your hands describes a number of scales and the strong chords that are associated with them. If you stick to the chords listed for each scale you can't go wrong (if I'm right).

The chord groups are either JRM Loose or JRM Strict. These terms are explained later. Check out my book John's Rules Music which describes the difference between JRM Loose and JRM Strict...

www.johnsmusic7.com/JohnsRulesMusic.pdf

Chapter One
Eagle Fretted Guitars

First of all, if you want to play Eagle 53 music on a guitar you will need an Eagle fretted guitar. There are specifications for fret placements listed below. You could hire a luthier to build an Eagle fretted guitar from scratch but it would be simpler, faster and cheaper to buy a guitar and then modify its fretboard yourself (or hire a luthier to do the re-fretting).

Over the years I have done a few refrets (I am not a luthier). I would buy a cheap guitar, rip out the frets, fill the slots with wood cement or resin, saw new slots for the new frets and then fit the new frets. This is not easy, especially for the inexperienced, so I recommend hiring a luthier to do the refret for you if you can afford it.

Below are lists of distances from the nut for each fret according to each of the 12 keys. The 'y' indicates the *scale length* of the guitar which is the distance from the nut to the saddle on the lightest string. The saddle is usually angled slightly so that the distance from the nut to the saddle is slightly longer for the lower, thicker strings. I go to seven decimal places in these lists but this degree of precision is unnecessary. A half millimetre or 1/64 inch accuracy should be fine.

Key 1 (E)...0.0632991y, 0.111041y, 0.167311y, 0.199349y, 0.25003y, 0.288254y, 0.333307y, 0.375508y, 0.399535y, 0.444852y, 0.466212y, 0.5y, 0.53165y, 0.555521y, 0.583656y, 0.599675y, 0.625015y, 0.644127y, 0.666654y, 0.687754y, 0.699768y, 0.722426y, 0.733106y, 0.75y.

Key 2 (F)...0.0509683y, 0.111041y, 0.145244y, 0.199349y, 0.240157y, 0.288254y, 0.333307y, 0.358958y, 0.407337y, 0.43014y, 0.466212y, 0.5y, 0.525484y, 0.555521y, 0.572622y, 0.599675y, 0.620078y, 0.644127y, 0.666654y, 0.679479y, 0.703669y, 0.71507y, 0.733106y, 0.75y.

Key 3 (F#)...0.063299y, 0.0993387y, 0.15635y, 0.199349y, 0.25003y, 0.297502y, 0.324531y, 0.375508y, 0.399535y, 0.437544y, 0.473147y, 0.5y, 0.531649y, 0.549669y, 0.578175y, 0.599675y, 0.625015y, 0.648751y, 0.662265y, 0.687754y, 0.699768y, 0.718772y, 0.736574y, 0.75y.

Key 4 (G)...0.0384751y, 0.0993388y, 0.145244y, 0.199349y, 0.25003y, 0.278885y, 0.333307y, 0.358958y, 0.399536y, 0.437544y, 0.466212y, 0.5y, 0.519238y, 0.549669y, 0.572622y, 0.599675y, 0.625015y, 0.639442y, 0.666654y, 0.679479y, 0.699768y, 0.718772y, 0.733106y, 0.75y.

Key 5 (G#)...0.0632991y, 0.111041y, 0.167311y, 0.22002y, 0.25003y, 0.30663y, 0.333307y, 0.375508y, 0.415038y, 0.444852y, 0.479993y, 0.5y, 0.53165y, 0.555521y, 0.583656y, 0.61001y, 0.625015y, 0.653315y, 0.666654y, 0.687754y, 0.707519y, 0.722426y, 0.739996y, 0.75y.

Key 6 (A)...0.0509682y, 0.111041y, 0.167311y, 0.199349y, 0.259774y, 0.288254y, 0.333307y, 0.375508y, 0.407337y, 0.444852y, 0.466212y, 0.5y, 0.525484y, 0.555521y, 0.583656y, 0.599675y, 0.629887y, 0.644127y, 0.666654y, 0.687754y, 0.703669y, 0.722426y, 0.733106y, 0.75y.

Key 7 (A#)...0.0632991y, 0.122591y, 0.15635y, 0.22002y, 0.25003y, 0.297502y, 0.341969y, 0.375508y, 0.415038y, 0.437544y, 0.473147y, 0.5y, 0.53165y, 0.561296y, 0.578175y, 0.61001y, 0.625015y, 0.648751y, 0.670985y, 0.687754y, 0.707519y, 0.718772y, 0.736574y, 0.75y.

Key 8 (B)...0.0632991y, 0.0993387y, 0.167311y, 0.199349y, 0.25003y, 0.297502y, 0.333307y, 0.375508y, 0.399535y, 0.437544y, 0.466212y, 0.5y, 0.53165y, 0.549669y, 0.583656y, 0.599675y, 0.625015y, 0.648751y, 0.666654y, 0.687754y, 0.699768y, 0.718772y, 0.733106y, 0.75y.

Key 9 (C)...0.0384751y, 0.111041y, 0.145244y, 0.199349y, 0.25003y, 0.288254y, 0.333307y, 0.358958y, 0.399535y, 0.43014y, 0.466212y, 0.5y, 0.519238y, 0.555521y, 0.572622y, 0.599675y, 0.625015y, 0.644127y, 0.666654y, 0.679479y, 0.699768y, 0.71507y, 0.733106y, 0.75y.

Key 10 (C#)...0.0754697y, 0.111041y, 0.167311y, 0.22002y, 0.259774y, 0.30663y, 0.333307y, 0.375508y, 0.407337y, 0.444852y, 0.479993y, 0.5y, 0.537735y, 0.555521y, 0.583656y, 0.61001y, 0.629887y, 0.653315y, 0.666654y, 0.687754y, 0.703669y, 0.722426y, 0.739996y, 0.75y.

Key 11 (D)...0.0384751y, 0.0993387y, 0.15635y, 0.199349y, 0.25003y, 0.278885y, 0.324531y, 0.358958y, 0.399535y, 0.437544y, 0.459185y, 0.5y, 0.519238y, 0.549669y, 0.578175y, 0.599675y, 0.625015y, 0.639442y, 0.662265y, 0.679479y, 0.699768y, 0.718772y, 0.729592y, 0.75y.

Key 12 (D#)...0.0632991y, 0.122591y, 0.167311y, 0.22002y, 0.25003y, 0.297502y, 0.333307y, 0.375508y, 0.415038y, 0.437544y, 0.479993y, 0.5y, 0.53165y, 0.561296y, 0.583656y, 0.61001y, 0.625015y, 0.648751y, 0.666654y, 0.687754y, 0.707519y, 0.718772y, 0.739996y, 0.75y.

For a guitar tuned EADGBE use the fret distances listed in keys 1, 6, 11, 4, 8, and 1 again (corresponds to EADGBE). The frets will look like this...

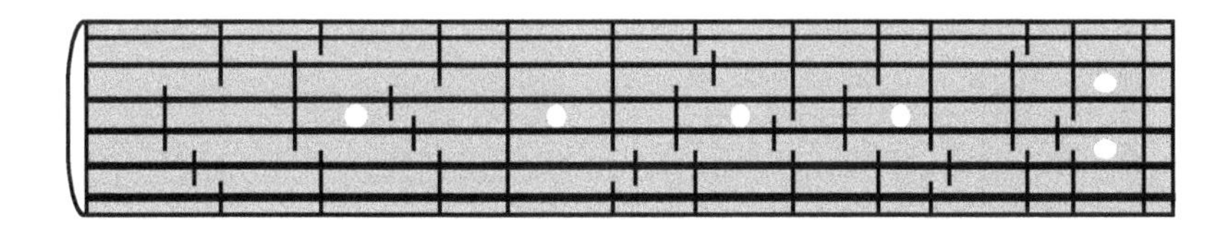

Chapter Two
Eagle Tuned Keyboards

If you have an acoustic piano you will need to retune it to the Eagle 53 tuning. I propose using the frequency of a standard 12TET E note as the base frequency for Eagle 53. So E is 164.8138 Hz, or an octave higher 329.6276 Hz, or an octave higher again 659.2551 Hz and so on. With lower octaves the values are halved instead of doubled.

Below are the frequencies of Eagle 53 notes over a one octave range (between 164.81378 Hz and 329.62756 Hz)

```
E    164.81 Hz
F    164.81 Hz x 1.06758 = 175.95 Hz
F#   164.81 Hz x 1.12491 = 185.40 Hz
G    164.81 Hz x 1.20093 = 197.93 Hz
G#   164.81 Hz x 1.24898 = 205.85 Hz
A    164.81 Hz x 1.33339 = 219.76 Hz
A#   164.81 Hz x 1.405   = 231.56 Hz
B    164.81 Hz x 1.49994 = 247.21 Hz
C    164.81 Hz x 1.6013  = 263.92 Hz
C#   164.81 Hz x 1.66538 = 274.48 Hz
D    164.81 Hz x 1.80132 = 296.88 Hz
D#   164.81 Hz x 1.8734  = 308.76 Hz
E    164.81 Hz x 2.0     = 329.63 Hz
```

For higher octave ranges multiply each result here by 2, 4, 8, 16 etc. For lower octave ranges divide each result by 2, 4, 8, 16 etc. I chose 164.81378 Hz (a standard 12TET E note) as my base frequency but you can choose any base frequency you like and multiply it in a similar fashion to the above.

Many professional piano tuners “stretch tune” pianos. If I remember correctly all intervals are tuned slightly wider than you would expect mathematically. I don’t know much about this subject but for me, to keep things simple, I would stick with the frequencies listed above.

Most modern electric keyboards can be connected to, and controlled by, a computer. You will need to acquire a special cable, or interface, to connect your keyboard to your computer. You will also need special software to retune your keyboard. I use microsynth-mini by H-Pi Instruments which is very reasonably priced for what you get. There are versions for both Windows and Mac. I think there are some free tuning programs available on the internet.

You will need to set the tuning you want using the software you have. Here are the adjustments in cents (a cent is one hundredth of a standard 12TET semitone).

```
E      0.0 cents, same as usual
F    113.2 cents, 13.2 cents higher than usual
F#   203.8 cents, 3.8 cents higher than usual
G    317.0 cents, 17 cents higher than usual
G#   384.9 cents, 15.1 cents lower than usual
A    498.1 cents, 1.9 cents lower than usual
A#   588.7 cents, 11.3 cents lower than usual
B    701.9 cents, 1.9 cents higher than usual
C    815.1 cents, 15.1 cents higher than usual
C#   883.0 cents, 17 cents lower than usual
D   1018.9 cents, 18.9 cents higher than usual
D# 1086.8 cents, 13.2 cents lower than usual
```

If you need assistance setting up your computer and retuning your keyboard I recommend these two Facebook groups which are devoted primarily to alternatively tuned music and the theory behind it...

Microtonal Music and Tuning Theory
www.facebook.com/groups/497105067092502

The Xenharmonic Alliance
www.facebook.com/groups/xenharmonic2

Chapter Three
My Favourite
Chord Progression

C	C	C7	C7
F	F	F7	F7
C	Am	F	G
C	F	C	G

Count two beats to each bar.

Is this type of progression playable in Eagle 53? Yes it is, on one key only: the key of C if E is 1/1.

The progression is not JRM strict (more on JRM later). The C7 chord has an A# which does not pair nicely, melodically, with the F note. Also the F7 chord has a D note which does not pair nicely, melodically, with the A note. This chord progression is JRM loose. All the chords are strongly rooted (except the Am chord). Looking at the root notes of the strongly rooted chords and looking at all the notes in the Am chord, all of these notes pair nicely with each other melodically so the progression should be acceptable. JRM Loose.

I propose two (there are others) scales that can be used to play 'lead' over the chords. One is the pentatonic minor....

C, D#, F, G, A#, C

Over the one octave range between the low C and the high C all the notes in this scale pair nicely with each other melodically. Outside the one octave range an occasional sour melodic note occurs. The A# does not pair nicely, melodically, with the F note just *above* it. A# does pair nicely, melodically, with the F note just *below* it (in Eagle 53).

The other scale is C, E, F, G, A, C. I don't have a name for it. The notes are good melodically over *any* range.

The F7 chord (near the nut) is impossible to play on my Eagle 53 fretted guitar. I suggest using
Ex, Ax, D3, G2, B4, Ex (F, A, D#) instead.
Ax means don't play a note on the A string.
D3 means play the note at the third fret on the D string (this is an F note).

F7 substitute chord (F, A, D#) on E53 guitar is...
E---x
B---4
G---2
D---3
A---x
E---x

Again: Ax means don't play a note on the A string.
D3 means play the note at the third fret on the D string.
Here are all the chords in the progression...

C - C, E, G, C, E
E---0
B---1
G---0
D---2
A---3
E---x

C7 - C, E, A#, C, E
E---0
B---1
G---3
D---2
A---3
E---x

F - F, C, F, A, C, F
E---1
B---1
G---2
D---3
A---3
E---1

F7 - F, A, D#
E---x
B---4
G---2
D---3
A---x
E---x

Am - A, E, A, C, E
E---0
B---1
G---2
D---2
A---0
E---x

G - G, D, G, B, D, G
E---3
B---3
G---4
D---5
A---5
E---3

Chapter Four
The D+ scale

When I began working with Eagle 53 I noticed that most of the common open chords occur (are in tune and are more in tune than in 12TET). E major, E minor, G major, A major, A minor, C major occur in Eagle 53 but there is no major or minor chord available on D.

In 12 Tone Equal Temperament open D major and minor chords occur. The D in 12TET makes a 16/9 over the bottom E note. The D in Eagle 53 is different. It makes a 9/5 over the bottom E. So it sounds a bit different to what you are used to.

I discovered a 6:10:12:15 (D, B, D, F#) open chord on D. As I said, it functions differently to a 12TET D chord but it definitely works in the right context (the right scale).

Here is a scale built to accommodate the 6:10:12:15 D chord...

E, F#, G, A#, B, C, D, E

I call it The D+ (D plus) scale.

Here are some chords that conform to this scale...

E major
F# 4:5:8:10 (F#, A#, F#, A#)
G major
A# 7:10:14:20 (A#, E, A#, E)
B minor
C major
D+ 6:10:12:15 (D, B, D, F#)

All of these chords should make good progressions over *any* range (excluding very low, bass registers where single notes work better than chords).

Chapter Five
JRM Strict Chord Progressions

Below are six chord progressions that begin on E. The progressions are JRM Strict meaning that every note in every chord pairs nicely with every other note melodically. All of the notes in each chord group belong to the scale listed just above them.
JS stands for JRM Strict

JS1 - E F F# G A B C D# E

E minor
F major
G 4:5:8:10 (G, B, G, B)
A minor
B major
C major

JS2 - E F F# G# A B C D# E

E major
F major
G# minor
A minor
B major
C 4:5:8:10 (C, E, C, E)

JS3 - E F G A B C# D# E

E minor
F 4:5:8:10 (F, A, F, A)
G 4:5:8:10 (G, B, G, B)
A major
B 4:5:8:10 (B, D#, B, D#)

JS4 - E F G# A B C# D# E

E major
F 4:5:8:10 (F, A, F, A)
G# minor
A major
B 4:5:8:10 (B, D#, B, D#)
C# minor

JS5 - E F# G A A# B C D# E

E minor
F# 4:5:8:10 (F#, A#, F#, A#)
G 4:5:8:10 (G, B, G, B)
A minor
A# 7:10:14:20 (A#, E, A#, E)
B major
C major
D# minor

JS6 - E F# G# A A# B C D# E

E major
F# 4:5:8:10 (F#, A#, F#, A#)
G# minor
A minor
B major
C 4:5:8:10 (C, E, C, E)
D# minor

All of these chords above should make good progressions over *any* range (excluding very low, bass registers) where single notes work better than chords).

You will have to do a listening test to identify which, if any, chord functions as a tonic, a point of resolution, a point of rest in each group.

Chapter Six
Beatless chords and JRM Loose progressions

For an elucidation of beats/beating check out the last page of chapter two in my book: John's Rules Music
A free PDF of the book is available here...
www.johnsmusic7.com/JohnsRulesMusic.pdf

When I use the term "beatless chord" I refer to chords that have no *noticeable* beating for *my* ear. What is beatless for me may not be beatless for others.

The chord progressions here are not JRM strict (because some notes clash melodically with others) but each chord is beatless (and in my view, pure) and is very strongly rooted (except the A# chord which is beatless but not strongly rooted). I think that if the root notes of each strongly rooted chord in a given progression (of strongly rooted chords only) pair nicely with each other then the progression should be acceptable. The other notes (not the root notes) in each chord don't matter (see my JRM book for more on this).

I consider every interval (apart from the unison, 1/1) narrower than 5/4 to have some noticeable beating (which I find unpleasant). For me this applies to the fundamentals and first overtones of the two notes in any interval. For example the 13/7 interval is wide but the first overtone of the 7 (which is 14) beats against the fundamental of the 13, a very narrow interval (14/13). For me the second and subsequent overtones are too faint to be significant. See my JRM book for more on this.

Using an Eagle fretted guitar you could omit the highest note in each chord below for easier playing.
Here are the strongest beatless chords that occur in Eagle 53...

```
E   2:3:4:6     E, B, E, B
F   2:3:4:6     F, C, F, C
F# 4:5:8:10    F#, A# F#, A#
G   2:3:4:6     G, D, G, D
G# 2:3:4:6     G#, D#, G#, D#
A   2:3:4:6     A, E, A, E
A# 7:10:14:20 A#, E, A#, E
B   2:3:4:6     B, F#, B, F#
C   2:3:4:6     C, G, C, G
C# 2:3:4:6     C#, G#, C#, G#
D   4:5:8:10    D, F#, D, F#
D# 2:3:4:6     D#, A#, D#, A#
```

Below are seven beatless chord Progressions. The 'B' stand for beatless.

B1 - E F F# G A B C D# E

E 2:3:4:6 E, B, E, B
F 2:3:4:6 F, C, F, C
F# 4:5:8:10 F#, A# F#, A#
G 2:3:4:6 G, D, G, D
A 2:3:4:6 A, E, A, E
B 2:3:4:6 B, F#, B, F#
C 2:3:4:6 C, G, C, G
D# 2:3:4:6 D#, A#, D#, A#

I, IV, V major chords progression is available on if C is used as the tonic.

B2 - E F F# G# A B C D# E

E 2:3:4:6 E, B, E, B
F 2:3:4:6 F, C, F, C
F# 4:5:8:10 F#, A# F#, A#
G# 2:3:4:6 G#, D#, G#, D#
A 2:3:4:6 A, E, A, E
B 2:3:4:6 B, F#, B, F#
C 2:3:4:6 C, G, C, G
D# 2:3:4:6 D#, A#, D#, A#

B3 - E F G A B C# D# E

E 2:3:4:6 E, B, E, B
F 2:3:4:6 F, C, F, C
G 2:3:4:6 G, D, G, D
A 2:3:4:6 A, E, A, E
B 2:3:4:6 B, F#, B, F#
C# 2:3:4:6 C#, G#, C#, G#
D# 2:3:4:6 D#, A#, D#, A#

B4 -E F G# A B C# D# E

E 2:3:4:6 E, B, E, B
F 2:3:4:6 F, C, F, C
G# 2:3:4:6 G#, D#, G#, D#
A 2:3:4:6 A, E, A, E
B 2:3:4:6 B, F#, B, F#
C# 2:3:4:6 C#, G#, C#, G#
D# 2:3:4:6 D#, A#, D#, A#

B5 - E F# G A A# B C D# E

E 2:3:4:6 E, B, E, B
F# 4:5:8:10 F#, A# F#, A#
G 2:3:4:6 G, D, G, D
A 2:3:4:6 A, E, A, E
A# 7:10:14:20 A#, E, A#, E
B 2:3:4:6 B, F#, B, F#
C 2:3:4:6 C, G, C, G
D# 2:3:4:6 D#, A#, D#, A#

B6 - E F# G# A A# B C D# E

E 2:3:4:6 E, B, E, B
F# 4:5:8:10 F#, A# F#, A#
G# 2:3:4:6 G#, D#, G#, D#
A 2:3:4:6 A, E, A, E
A# 7:10:14:20 A#, E, A#, E
B 2:3:4:6 B, F#, B, F#
C 2:3:4:6 C, G, C, G
D# 2:3:4:6 D#, A#, D#, A#

B7 (contains a D chord)
E F# G A# B C D E

E 2:3:4:6 E, B, E, B
F# 4:5:8:10 F#, A# F#, A#
G 2:3:4:6 G, D, G, D
A# 7:10:14:20 A#, E, A#, E
B 2:3:4:6 B, F#, B, F#
C 2:3:4:6 C, G, C, G
D 4:5:8:10 D, F#, D, F#

All of these chords above should make good progressions over *any* range (excluding very low, bass registers where single notes work better than chords). So the chords listed above could be played over, say, a four octave or more range if desired. The root notes do not have to be confined to a one octave range.

You will have to do a listening test to identify which, if any, chord functions as a tonic, a point of resolution, a point of rest in each chord group.

Chapter Seven
Miscellany

Playing Lead Over the Chords

There is a scale associated with each group of chords listed above. I suspect that the notes in each scale will sound good if played as 'lead' over the relevant chords. The lead notes should be good if the notes belong to the scale chosen. I haven't tested this idea yet.

Tonic or Root Chords

The root or tonic chord in any progression is not always the lowest chord. You have to do a listening test yourself to decide which chord, if any, is a point of resolution, a point of rest.

Ranges of Chords

Most, if not all, of the chord progressions described in this book are good over *any* range, not just over one octave.

Chapter Eight
My Other Books

All of my paperback books are available on Amazon but sometimes a book will be listed on Amazon as "currently unavailable". If this is the case then go to www.barnesandnoble.com in the US or www.waterstones.com in the UK instead and the book you want will hopefully be on sale there.

———

Some Observations on the King James Bible
(ISBN 9781838121976)

This book highlights some seemingly nonsensical verses, contradictions and inconsistencies that I came across when reading the standard King James Version of The Holy Bible. These prove (to me at least) that the Holy Bible is *not* the infallible, and inerrant, Word of God.

A free PDF of the book is here...

www.johnsmusic7.com/sootkjb.pdf

If the book is unavailable on Amazon go to...
www.barnesandnoble.com in the US
or www.waterstones.com in the UK instead.

The John O'Sullivan Diet Fruit and Nuts
(ISBN 9781838121983)

This book advocates a vegan diet with an emphasis on fruit and nuts for the purposes of health and healing.

I have written and published nine other books about the Eagle 53 tuning. These books are all available on Amazon and some other online booksellers. If you are interested here are the details...

Eagle 53 My Ultimate Musical Tuning
ISBN 9780956649294

This book describes how I arrived at Eagle 53, the math and the rationale behind it.

John's Rules Music
ISBN 9781838121921

Rules for music composition in regular tuning, my Eagle 53 tuning, or any other alternative tuning. A free PDF of the book is available here.... www.johnsmusic7.com/JohnsRulesMusic.pdf

----

The Eagle 53 Pianist
ISBN 9781838121907

Eagle 53 Jazz Chords
ISBN 9781838121914

The two books above are for players of pianos or keyboards tuned to Eagle 53.

The Eagle 53 Guitarist Lush Chords
ISBN 9781838121938

The Eagle 53 Guitarist Jazz Chords
ISBN 9781838121945

These two books above are for guitarists who have guitars fretted for Eagle 53.

The Arabian Scale in Eagle 53
ISBN 9781838121952

This is for Eagle 53 guitarists or keyboard players. It lists 507 chords that, if I'm right, will all sound good played in any order.

Eagle 53 Beatless Lutes and 19EDO
ISBN 9781838121969

This is two short books rolled into one. Players of fretted and stringed instruments (e.g. guitar, banjo, ukulele, mandolin) might find book 1 interesting and people into math and tuning theory might find book 2 interesting. And some luthiers will be interested in both books.

The Swan Scale in Eagle 53
ISBN 9781739407407

2,000 chords that conform to the Swan scale
in Eagle 53. This book is intended for
keyboard players.

This eBook is cheap and available on Amazon...
The name of the eBook is: "Eagle 53 Musical Tuning"

Magic Mushrooms An Autobiography
ISBN 9781838121990

My short autobiography

As I said: if a book is unavailable on Amazon then go to www.barnesandnoble.com in the US or www.waterstones.com in the UK instead.

Afterword

There may be a few errors in this book. It's hard to get it right all the time.

For a demonstration of a chord progression (36 chords) where every note in every chord pairs nicely, melodically, with every other note (JRM Strict) check out this web app that I wrote...

www.johnsmusic7.com/swan.html

Here's a another app with beatless chords...

www.johnsmusic7.com/heart.html

There is a lot more information on my tuning system on my website…

www.johnsmusic7.com

Go vegan!
It will be good for you,
good for the animals
and good for the planet!

I support PETA (People for the Ethical Treatment of Animals).
Check out their website...

www.peta.org

John O'Sullivan

26th July, 2023

Milton Keynes UK
Ingram Content Group UK Ltd.
UKHW020917100823
426648UK00010B/37